When your puppy gets hungry, **feed him some yummy food.**

Make your puppy **sit, jump and bark!**

Play with your puppy – he loves fetching and getting treats as a reward.

Explore the app to learn more facts and tricks, and become a **puppy expert.**

★ ★ ★ ★ ★

THIS IS A CARLTON BOOK

Published in 2018 by Carlton Books Limited, an imprint of the Carlton Publishing Group, 20 Mortimer Street, London W1T 3JW

A catalogue record for this book is available from the British Library.

ISBN: 978-1-78312-347-6

Printed in Dongguan, China

1 3 5 7 9 10 8 6 4 2

Written by: Kay Woodward
Executive Editors: Alexandra Koken and Stephanie Stahl
Design Manager: Emily Clarke
Design: Ceri Hurst
Picture research: Steve Behan
Production: Emma Smart

★ ★ ★ ★ ★

The publishers would like to thank the following sources for their kind permission to reproduce the pictures in this book.

T=top, B=bottom, C=centre, L=left, R=right.

Getty Images: /Nick Ridley: 24TL, 32BL; /Alessandra Sarti: 28BR; /Philip Thompson/EyeEm: 4TR, 7; /Sharon Vos-Arnold: 1TR, 8TL

Ceri Hurst: 4TC, 32BR

Shutterstock: /Adya: 1BL, 13T, 16BR; /andrixph: 30BC; /anetapics: 24R; /antoniodiaz: 18R; /ArtdayAnna: 11BL, 32TL; /Asichka: 23TR; /Mila Atkovska: 6TL; /BG-FOTO: 9TL; /Ihor Berkyta: 30TL; /Javier Brosch: 20TL; /Andrew Burgess: 2L, 11TL; /dekolaine: 5C; /EmilyRj: 28TL; /Natalia Fadosova: 16TL; /Golden Pixels LLC: 14BR, 15R; /Mat Hayward: 5TL, 12TL, 32TR; /Anna Hoychuk: 1TC, 22TL, 30C; /Ian 2010: 27TR; /Eric Isselee: 26-27B, 30BL; /Kalamurzing: 1BR, 10TL, 17TR; /Grigorita Ko: 22B; /Kirill Kurashov: 26TL; /Mariana Marakhovskaia: 22-23T, 30BR; /Maximilian100: 14TL; /Claire McAdams: 10B; /Andrii Muzyka: 12B; /pipicato: 1TL, 3R, 4C, 9TR, 17BR; /PriceM: 25; /Raevskaya: 4TL, 18TL; /schubbel: 29; /Stockimo: 21; /wavebreakmedia: 8R; /Dora Zett: 20R

Every effort has been made to acknowledge correctly and contact the source and/or copyright holder of each picture and Carlton Books Limited apologises for any unintentional errors or omissions, which will be corrected in future editions of this book.

My Perfect
Puppy

Kay Woodward

CARLTON KiDS

IT'S PUPPY TIME!

 Have you always wanted a dog? Well, guess what? You'll never have to wish for one again! You're just seconds away from meeting your very own perfect pup.

WHAT COLOUR IS YOUR PUPPY?

★ ★ ★ ★ ★

Choose the colour of your new puppy.

DESIGN YOUR OWN PUPPY

You're going to absolutely love your new puppy! Will it be a golden girl, a chocolate pup, a patchy boy, a spotty-dotty girl, a black beauty or a brown-and-white puppy? Trigger the Augmented Reality, choose your pet's colour and get ready to meet your PERFECT PUPPY!

Come back, Marmaduke!

NAMING TIME!

Your perfect puppy needs his very own name. You could choose a super-cute name like Fluffy or Sweetie Pie, or something more down-to-earth, like Rex or Barney. The most important thing is that you love the name! But it's also a good idea to pick something that you don't mind shouting at 100 decibels across a crowded park.

WHO'S IN THE BOX?
★ ★ ★ ★ ★
It's time to meet your new BFF!

Tap the box...

HELLO, PUPPY!

Imagine you're a puppy. Would you like it if a great grinning giant patted your head as if it were a basketball? No? Well, puppies aren't too keen on that either. What they *do* like is to be petted in just the right way.

When a puppy leans towards you, this is code for: PLEASE DON'T STOP PETTING ME.

TOP TIPS FOR PETTING A PUP

Puppies like to make friends with you, not the other way round. So crouch down and wait for the puppy to wag his tail and say hello. When he does, pet away! DO slowly pet your pup's shoulders or around his neck and chest, but DON'T pet the top of the head, the muzzle, tail, paws, legs and ears. And definitely DON'T hold a big, scary hand over his head.

HOW TO SPOT A HAPPY PUPPY

If you'd like to know whether your puppy is happy or sad, just look at him. If he backs away, licks his lips or shows the whites of his eyes, he's not in the best mood. But if your puppy puts his ears back and wags his tail, then he's H–A–P–P–Y. Hurray!

TOP TIP

Happy puppies are easy to spot. They look as if someone just told them that the world is made of dog biscuits.

★★★★★ **PETTING TIME** ★★★★★

Stroke, tickle or scratch your puppy, and he will be the happiest of all.

Use one finger to rub his ear...

Slowly swipe to stroke him...

Rub his belly to tickle him...

Then scratch his chin!

A PERFECT MATCH

Now for the really fun part. It's time to choose all the super-useful accessories that your new pet will need, like a cool collar and a funky nametag. Take your time because your puppy will have these for ever.

Some puppies suit wild and wacky accessories. Some puppies don't.

COLLAR

Take a good look at your perfect pup. What sort of personality do you think he might have? A green collar might suit bright, happy puppies. Calmer puppies would perhaps look better in blue. Will a puppy called Bandit look right with a bright red collar...? Hey, why not?

NAMETAG

All dogs need a nametag in case they get lost and your perfect puppy is no exception. Choose a nametag shape and colour. As soon as you've made your choice, your puppy's name will appear on the new nametag, just like magic!

ABRACADABRA

PUPPY STYLE

★ ★ ★ ★ ★

Your pup will look his very best with some fabulous accessories.

Choose one of these nametags...

...then pick a collar that will be perfect for your BFF.

SIT AND STAND!

Puppies are mischievous bundles of fun. They play and race, jump and bounce until they run out of energy, then they simply snooze. Teach your puppy to behave when he's young, then he will *always* be obedient.

Puppies are 100 per cent fun.
(But this doesn't mean they can't behave, too.)

YOUR PUP'S VERY FIRST LESSON

Start by teaching your pup to sit. All you need is a lot of patience and yummy treats... First, get down to your puppy's level. Hold a treat right in front of his nose. Say, 'SIT'. Then slowly lift the treat up into the air. And here's the really magic bit. As the puppy's nose goes up, his bottom will go down. Give him a treat and repeat this a few times — soon your pup will sit whenever you ask!

Sheepdogs must learn to be very obedient as they are used to control entire flocks of sheep.

DOWNS AND UPS

Hold a treat near your pup's nose and then move it downwards, while saying, 'DOWN'. When your pet is flat on the ground, give him the treat. Practise this until he recognises the brand-new word. You can use the same training technique to teach your pup to 'STAND' too!

Treat time!

★★★★★ **TIME TO LEARN** ★★★★★

Teach your pup how to sit, lie down and stand, and give him a treat when he gets it right.

Using two fingers...

Swipe down once...

Swipe down twice...

Swipe up...

STAY AND GO!

Your puppy has mastered the most basic commands. Well done, pup! Now it's time to teach him the slightly trickier stuff. Once your puppy has learnt these commands, you'll be able to take him anywhere!

This perfectly behaved pup LOVES dog biscuits!

BACK TO SCHOOL

'Stay' is one of the trickiest commands for a puppy to learn because he reeeeeally wants to run around and play. Put your pup on a lead and ask him to sit beside you. Then raise your hand and say, 'STAY'. Move away from your puppy, count to three and then move back. If he has stayed where he was, give him a treat. If he follows you, repeat the process until he gets it right.

PUPPY TRAINING

★★★★★

Train your furry friend to stay, go, come back and stop barking, and don't forget to give him a reward.

Tap with two fingers to stay...

Swipe right with two fingers to go...

Swipe left with two fingers to come back...

Woof!

Press down two fingers for a few seconds and your puppy will stop barking.

GOOD DOGS

The secret to a well-behaved puppy is praise — and lots of it! Never get cross when a puppy does something wrong. But when he does something positive, even if it's the tiniest thing ever, shower him with praise! Your puppy will soon be behaving PERFECTLY.

PUPPY TRICKS

Have you ever seen a puppy play the trombone? Of course not. You probably haven't seen him do a cartwheel either. But there are plenty of other skills and tricks that puppies can have fun learning. And the best bit is that you can teach them!

Give your puppy plenty of praise after he performs a trick. Then he'll want to do it again. And again.

Don't forget the treat!

TRICKS FOR BEGINNERS

An easy way to start is by asking your pup to 'LIFT A PAW'. (Don't forget to shake it.) Another fun trick for your puppy is to 'PLAY DEAD'. (He is not *actually* dead. This just means lying perfectly still.) While your puppy is flat on the ground, you can also teach him to 'ROLL OVER'.

AMAZING TRICKS

★ ★ ★ ★ ★

Your puppy is keen to learn some tricks such as lift a paw, roll over, sit pretty and stand on hind legs.

Swipe left with three fingers...

Draw a circle with three fingers...

Swipe up with three fingers...

Swipe down with three fingers...

SUPER-SLICK TRICKS

Now your puppy has learnt all the basic moves, it's time for more advanced tricks! Ask him to sit and then to lift up both front paws at the same time. This is called 'SITTING PRETTY'. The next trick is harder still. By holding a treat in the air, see if you can teach your pup to stand on his hind legs!

MMM...

Puppies will chew ANYTHING: curtains, rugs, the bedside table or even your granddad's favourite slippers! This is sometimes because they are teething, like babies, or they might just be bored.

YUM!

Puppies aren't fussy about what they chew. Trainers are just as chewable as dog biscuits!

THE NICE LIST

Being a puppy is hungry work! Feed yours three or four small meals a day to make sure he always has plenty of energy. But did you know that he doesn't *just* have to eat dog food? Puppies can also enjoy these delicious foods: watermelon, blueberries, strawberries, carrots, green beans, bananas and cooked chicken. (But not all at once!)

THE NAUGHTY LIST

There are some things that a puppy should NEVER EVER eat. Salty snacks, raw meat, mouldy food, bones, corn on the cob, raw eggs, milk, stinky cheese, avocados, grapes, raisins, anything citrusy, onions, garlic, chives, macadamia nuts and coconuts are all banned. And if you ever see your puppy drinking a chocolate milkshake, take it off him at once!

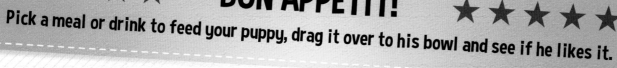

BON APPETIT!

Pick a meal or drink to feed your puppy, drag it over to his bowl and see if he likes it.

★ ★ ★ ★ ★

TOP TIP

Chocolate might seem like a wonderful treat for your puppy, but it really, REALLY isn't! Save the chocolate for yourself and give him a carrot to munch instead!

WALKIES

Puppies are bouncing balls of energy and they love to play outside! They need lots and lots (and LOTS) of exercise. Take them out morning, noon and evening, and they'll love you always!

There are no prizes for guessing what this puppy would like to do.

When a puppy needs to go, he needs to go.

SUPER POOPERS

Puppies poo. A lot. So it's important to make sure that they poo in the right place (outside) and not the wrong place (your mum's handbag!). Remember to take a plastic bag with you to scoop the poo away. If you take out your puppy every day, he'll be house-trained in no time.

OUT AND ABOUT

★ ★ ★ ★ ★

Take your puppy out on a walk and see what he gets up to.

Your puppy loves splashing in puddles...

...and playing with mud!

Uh-oh! Your pup needs to go!

Now drag the poo bag into the bin.

> I love mud!

MUDDY PAWS

When puppies go wild in the countryside, they're just out to have fun. So if you want to keep the grown-ups happy, too, it's probably a good idea to clean your puppy's paws before he decorates the carpets with a beautiful paw-print pattern.

ZZZ

Did you know that some puppies need an astonishing *18 hours* of sleep a day? It's not because they're lazy. A puppy needs to sleep because he is busy growing. If he didn't sleep so much, he would be more likely to become ill or be in a bad mood.

Newborn puppies can sleep for over 21 hours a day!

NAPTIME

Puppies don't just sleep at night. During the daytime, they are napping champions! If your puppy suddenly turns super naughty, he hasn't had a personality change. He probably just needs a power nap. And if he's played fetch 157 times at the park, guess what he needs afterwards...? Bingo. Another nap.

Well, wouldn't you need a nap after this?

BEDTIME

Like babies, puppies may not sleep for the whole night through. Help your puppy to sleep by giving him a good run before bedtime. Has he been to the toilet? Good. Now make sure his bed is super cosy. And don't let him drink litres and litres of water just before going to bed or things could get messy!

This puppy is dreaming about sticks. (Probably.)

★ ★ ★ ★ ★ **GOODNIGHT!** ★ ★ ★ ★ ★

It's time for your puppy to go to sleep in his cosy bed.

Try tapping his mouth...

...his ear...

...his leg.

Or swipe up with two fingers to wake him up!

RUN, PUPPY, RUN!

Puppies love to run: FACT. But the last thing you want is your wonderful puppy galloping into the distance and disappearing over the horizon. By far the best way of letting him run safely is to play fetch.

Wheeeeeeeeeeeee!

FETCH!

Fetch is a brilliant way for your puppy to run and run and NOT get lost. Choose an object that flies through the air easily and that your puppy can hold in his jaws. A ball is perfect. A frisbee is even better. An inflatable dolphin is not so good! Take your chosen object to the park, pull back your arm and throw it as far as you can. Now get ready for the best puppy exercise ever.

PLAYFUL PUPPY

When you're playing fetch, remember three things. Firstly, your puppy may become distracted when he's running for the ball and bring back something else instead. Secondly, puppies dribble. A lot. So you may have to throw a very wet and sticky ball. If so, BE BRAVE. Thirdly, puppies want to play fetch for ever. But if he looks super tired, it's probably time to go home!

Yes, you really are going to have to throw this ball!

 **LET'S PLAY!**

Play fetch with your puppy - the perfect way to make sure he always comes back to you.

Swipe your finger to throw the ball and see if your pup brings it back.

Don't forget to use the other puppy tricks you have learnt to interact with your friend!

Remember to give him a treat!

TUG OF WAR!

Hmm. The weather outside is terrible, but your puppy is full of energy... What do you do? Simple. Play a game of tug of war with him! It's the perfect rainy-day activity for puppies.

There's only one thing that a puppy loves more than a game of tug of war... another game of tug of war!

GET KNOTTED

Find a short, thick rope. Tie a knot at each end, big enough for you to grasp and for your puppy to grip between his teeth. Next find a big enough space to play and make sure that you are nowhere near any beautiful china ornaments that used to belong to your great-great-great-grandmother.

This is so much fun!

PUPPY GAMES

★ ★ ★　　　　★ ★ ★

Your perfect puppy loves to play,
but what he loves the most is to play with YOU!

Pull the phone or tablet towards you to play tug of war with your puppy. Check the onscreen meter to see how you are both doing.

If your pup wins, give him a treat – he deserves it!

READY, STEADY... TUG!

Remember that you're the one in control — not your puppy. Only play tug of war in short bursts — 30 seconds is more than enough. If puppies play tug of war for a very long time, they could get so overexcited that they lose control. There's only one more very important rule that you absolutely must not ignore: HAVE FUN!

SOUND OF PUPPIES

Puppies don't *just* bark. They make all sorts of super cute noises. They moan and they sigh and they whine and they growl and they howl. But what do these sounds actually *mean*...?

HAPPY OR SAD?

Believe it or not, when a puppy moans, he *isn't* miserable. This is a sound that he usually makes when he is near his loved ones — either his dog family or his human family. (That includes you!) A sigh is another happy sound, unless the puppy's eyes are wide open. Then it means that the puppy is disappointed in you... (Oh dear.) Whines can be happy or sad. Howling is something that wolves do to communicate with the rest of their pack. Dogs do it, too!

This puppy is singing a song to all other puppies.

This puppy has been trained not to bark at kittens.

SHHH!

Some puppies bark at passers-by. Some bark at cats. Others bark at EVERYTHING. But you can teach them to stop. NEVER shout at your puppy. To him, this means you are just barking back. Don't react. Simply turn your back and wait for him to stop barking. Then, just like other kinds of puppy training, be sure to give your puppy LOTS of praise — and a treat.

★ ★ ★ ★ ★ **LET'S SING!** ★ ★ ★ ★ ★

Choose a song or just play the keyboard, and your puppy will sing along with you.

HOME SWEET HOME

 Now you've found out nearly all there is to know about puppies, except for one thing. Your adorable puppy needs somewhere to snuggle down! Make sure you pick just the right place for your pup to live.

Don't forget that your puppy will grow. Choose a bed that will fit when he's older, too.

HIS VERY OWN SPACE

Your puppy's bed is his refuge — the place he hides in when he wants a break. Does your puppy stretch out when he sleeps? If so, he will need a bigger bed. But if your pup curls up, then a small, comfy bed might be better.

A PLACE TO REST

Where does your puppy snuggle down? On a squishy cushion? In a dog bed? On *your* bed? (Shhh. Don't tell your parents.) Some dogs are lucky enough to have their very own kennel to sleep in. These can be very plain or very fancy.

Which kennel suits your dog best?